The Kingman Comprehension Series

Elementary Level 4

Dr. Alice Kingman

PARTRIDGE

To order additional copies of this book, contact
Toll Free +65 3165 7531 (Singapore)
Toll Free +60 3 3099 4412 (Malaysia)
orders.singapore@partridgepublishing.com

www.partridgepublishing.com/singapore

CONTENTS

CONTENTS

Acknowledgements

First, I would like to thank Jazzy, the illustrator of the Kingman Comprehension Series, for her beautiful artistic drawings which bring every story she has worked on to life.

My great appreciation is also to be extended to my two daughters, Stephanie and Audrey, who helped me from the very beginning in the typing and formatting of questions for every reading passage.

A big thank you to my beloved husband, Matt, for his continuous support, encouragement and professional assistance in the computerised structuring of the book.

I am also grateful to all my students for their contributions to this project, working on different passages, testing out questions and providing invaluable feedback.

With no reservation, my heartfelt gratitude goes to my beloved late father, Joseph, who spared no effort in teaching me English since I was seven years old.

Thank you to all other members of my family who spurred me on to take this big step in realising my dreams of becoming an English-language author. I thank them for their love and patience throughout the whole process.

Thank you to my wonderful church family as well for their uplifting prayers and support.

Last but not least, I thank God, my Heavenly Father, every day for His unfailing presence and spiritual guidance, without which this project would not have happened.

To Teacher and Parent

In my lifelong career as an English-language teacher, I have often been disappointed and discouraged to find questions set for comprehension passages stressing speedy location of answers or meticulous reproduction of the text. The formulated questions seldom encourage students to read between the lines or genuinely understand the writer's choice of diction and intention of writing. In other words, students are often deprived of opportunities to think out of the box and explore implied meanings and examine the purpose of sentence structure.

Hence, it has always been my ambition to produce a comprehension series that can sharpen students' skills in analytical discernment. The Kingman Comprehension Series comprises high-interest selections of different literary genres from classics to renowned children's literature including fables, folk and fairy tales, poems, legends, myths as well as modern realistic fictions. It is my hope that students will find the works of the outstanding authors in the books not only enjoyable to work on but also interesting enough to spark further independent reading among themselves.

About Angels

Laura E. Richards

"Mother," said the child, "are there really angels?"

"<u>The Good Book</u> says so," said the mother.

"Yes," said the child, "I have seen the picture. But did you ever see <u>one</u>, Mother?"

"I think I have," said the mother, "but she was not dressed like the picture."

"I am going to find one!" said the child. "I am going to run along the road, miles and miles and miles, until I find an angel."

"That will be a good plan!" said the mother. "And I will go with you, for you are too little to run far alone."

"I am not little anymore!" said the child. "I have trousers. I am big."

"So you are!" said the mother. "I forgot. But it is a fine day, and I should like the walk."

"But you walk so slowly with your lame foot."

"I can walk faster than you think!" said the mother.

So they started, the child leaping and running and the mother stepping out so bravely with her lame foot that the child soon forgot about it.

The child danced on ahead, and <u>presently,</u> he saw a chariot coming towards him, drawn by prancing white horses. In the chariot sat a splendid lady in velvet and furs, with white plumes waving above her dark hair. As she moved in her seat, she flashed with jewels and gold, but her eyes were brighter than her diamonds.

"Are you an angel?" asked the child, running up beside the chariot.

The lady made no reply but stared coldly at the child. Then she spoke a word to her coachman, and he flicked his whip, and the chariot rolled away swiftly in a cloud of dust and disappeared.

Answer the following questions.

1. "The Good Book" is referring to
   a. the Bible
   b. a very accurate book predicting the future
   c. an interesting book to read
   d. a book that is not bad

2. The underlined word "one" in the third line is referring to _____ _____.

3. Underline the sentence that shows the readers that the child was going a long, long way to find an angel.

4. According to the child, he was big because _____.

5. Why couldn't the child's mother walk fast?

6. Arrange the following sentences in the correct sequence:
   _____ The boy had seen the picture of an angel in the Good Book.
   _____ The boy asked his mother if angels really exist.
   _____ The boy's mother promised to go with him on his quest.
   _____ The boy announced that he was going to find an angel.

7. A synonym for the word "presently" is
   a. after a long while
   b. very soon
   c. at the present moment

8. Name three things the lady in the chariot was wearing.

9. Which two words indicate that the lady in the chariot was not friendly?

10. What do you think the lady in the chariot said to her coachman?

Read on:

'About Angels' is a short story found in *The Children's Book of Heroes* edited by William J. Bennet. The story begins with a young innocent child asking his mother if angels really exist. He then encounters two ladies of great charm and extravagance but eventually learns that external beauty and wealth do not make one an angel, but only the true love that a caring devoted mother would give to her child does.

Buster Bear Has a Fine Time

Thornton Burgess

Buster Bear was having the finest time he had had since he came down from the Great Woods to live in the Green Forest. To be sure, he wasn't in the Green Forest now, but he wasn't far from it. He was in the Old Pasture, one edge of which touches one edge of the Green Forest. And where do you think he was, in the Old Pasture? Why, right in the middle of the biggest patch of the biggest blueberries he ever had seen in all his life! Now if there is any one thing that Buster Bear had rather have above another, it is all the berries he can eat, unless it be honey. Nothing can be quite equal to honey in Buster's mind. But next to honey, give him berries. He isn't particular what kind of berries. Raspberries, blackberries, or blueberries, either kind, will make him perfectly happy.

"Um-m-m, my, my, but these are good!" he mumbled in his deep grumbly-rumbly voice, as he sat on his haunches stripping off the berries greedily. His little eyes twinkled with enjoyment, and he didn't mind at all if now and then he got leaves and some green berries in his mouth with the big ripe berries. He didn't try to get them out. Oh my, no! He just chomped <u>them</u> all up together and patted his stomach from sheer delight. Now Buster had reached the Old Pasture just as jolly, round, red Mr. Sun had crept out of bed, and he had fully made up his mind that he would be back in the Green Forest before Mr. Sun had climbed very far up in the blue, blue sky. You see, big as he is and strong as he is, Buster Bear is very shy and bashful, and he has no desire to meet Farmer Brown or Farmer Brown's boy or any other of those two-legged creatures called men. It seems funny, but he actually is afraid of them. And he had a feeling that he was a great deal more likely to meet one of them in the Old Pasture than deep in the Green Forest.

Answer the following questions.

1. Where did Buster Bear live before he came to live in the Green Forest?

2. Was the Old Pasture near the Green Forest? How do you know?

3. Which did Buster Bear like to eat more, berries or honey?

4. Would Buster Bear like to eat strawberries? Why do you think so?

5. Did Buster Bear exclaim loudly how good the blueberries were? Which word suggests that?

6. When one's eyes "twinkle," one is very
   a. happy
   b. bright
   c. artistic

7. The pronoun "them" in the sixth line of the second paragraph is referring to: _____, _____ _____ and _____.

8. Underline the phrase (three words in the second paragraph) that means "from pure joy."

9. How do we know the sun had come out when Buster reached the Old Pasture?

10. While Buster Bear was big and strong, he was also very _____ and _____.

11. Man was described as a two-legged creature because most other creatures had _____ _____.

12. Why would Buster Bear be more likely to meet man in the Old Pasture than the Green Forest?

Read on:

'Buster Bear Has a Fine Time' by Thornton W. Burgess follows one of the many adventures of the bashful but amiable Buster Bear that help children appreciate and respect animals and their natural habitats.

In the story, Buster Bear finds himself landed in a huge blueberry patch and is overwhelmed by a sudden craving for berries. He wanders from one patch to another, and the more he eats, the more he wants. Meanwhile, Mr. Sun in the sky is awaiting something funny to happen when Buster Bear and Farmer Brown's boy, who is filling his pail with blueberries, finally meet.

My Shadow

Robert Louis Stevenson

I have a little shadow that goes in and out with me,
And what can be the use of him is more than I can see.
He is very, very like me from the heels up to the head;
And I see him jump before me, when I jump into my bed.

The funniest thing about him is the way he likes to grow—
Not at all like proper children, which is always very slow;
For he sometimes shoots up taller like an india-rubber ball,
And he sometimes gets so little that there's none of him at all.

He hasn't got a notion of how children ought to play,
And can only make a fool of me in every sort of way.
He stays so close beside me, he's a coward you can see;
I'd think shame to stick to nursie as that shadow sticks to me!

One morning, very early, before the sun was up,
I rose and found the shining dew on every buttercup;
But my lazy little shadow, like an arrant sleepy-head,
Had stayed at home behind me and was fast asleep in bed.

Answer the following questions.

1. The poem "My Shadow" has four couplets/tercets/quatrains, containing four lines in each stanza.

2. What is the rhyme scheme of this poem?
   a. AABB
   b. ABAB
   c. ABBA

3. From whose point of view is the poem written?
   a. first person
   b. second person
   c. third person

4. Who is "he" as mentioned in the poem?

5. Compare the way proper children and the shadow grows?

6. Underline the expression (five words in the third stanza) which means "cause me to look silly."

7. In the third stanza, the speaker compares his shadow to _____ _____. Give a reason for that.

8. The poetic device we employ to give human characteristics to something that isn't human is called:
   a. simile
   b. metaphor
   c. personification

9. Which is not an example of the above poetic device in the poem?
   a. "And I see him jump before me," . . .
   b. "For he sometimes shoots up taller" . . .
   c. "I rose and found the shining dew on every buttercup."

10. Why couldn't the writer see the shadow early in the morning?

Read on:

The poem 'My Shadow,' written by Robert Louis Stevenson in 1885, portrays how a child gets fascinated and delighted as "another child" follows him everywhere, doing the same things he does. The acts the shadow does sometimes confuse the child though. The poem ends with the boy not being able to find his shadow one morning when he happens to get up before sunrise. 'My Shadow' is among Stevenson's most famous poems for children.

The Elves and the Servant Girl

The Brothers Grimm

There was once a poor servant girl who was industrious and cleanly and swept the house every day and emptied her sweepings on the great heap in front of the door. One morning, when she was just going back to her work, she found a letter on this heap, and as she could not read, she put her broom in the corner and took the letter to her master and mistress, and behold, it was an invitation from the elves, who asked the girl to hold a child for them at its christening. The girl did not know what to do, but at length, after much persuasion, and as they told her it was not right to refuse an invitation of this kind, she consented. Then three elves came and conducted her to a hollow mountain, where the little folks lived.

Everything there was small but more elegant and beautiful than can be described. The baby's mother lay in a bed of black ebony ornamented with pearls. The cover lids were embroidered with gold. The cradle was of ivory, the bath of gold. The girl stood as godmother and then wanted to go home again, but the little elves urgently entreated her to stay three days with them. So she stayed and passed the time in pleasure and gaiety, and the little folks did all they could to make her happy.

At last she set out on her way home. Then first, they filled her pockets quite full of money, and after that, they led her out of the mountain again. When she got home, she wanted to begin her work and took the broom, which was still standing in the corner, in her hand and began to sweep. Then some strangers came out of the house, who asked her who she was and what business she had there. And she had not, as she thought, been three days with the little men in the mountains but seven years, and in the meantime, her former masters had died.

Answer the following questions.

1. Which word in the first paragraph tells us that the servant girl is hardworking?

2. Where did the servant girl find the letter?

3. When a person cannot read and write, he or she is illegal/illegitimate/illiterate.

4. What was the request of the elves?

5. Did the girl accept the invitation of the elves? Which two words in the first paragraph suggest that?

6. Tick the three adjectives for describing the things inside the hollow mountain:
   a. small
   b. expensive
   c. elegant
   d. beautiful

7. Put the following in the correct sequence:
   _____ The elves led the girl to the mountain.
   _____ The girl was invited by the elves.
   _____ The girl wanted to go home.
   _____ The girl was made godmother.

8. Circle the odd word given below:
   a. pleasure
   b. gaiety
   c. happiness
   d. boredom

9. True or False:
   a. The elves asked the girl to stay for two days with them. _____
   b. The elves filled the pockets of the girl with jewels. _____
   c. The girl was ready to go back to her work upon arriving home. _____

10. What two questions did the stranger in the house ask the little girl?

11. How long did the girl think she was gone? How long was she really gone?

12. Is this story one of realism or fantasy?

Read on:

'The Elves and the Servant Girl' is the second story in the set of fairy tales collected by the Grimm Brothers in *The Elves and the Shoemaker*.

In the story, a poor servant girl is asked by the elves to act as the godparent at the baptism of one of their children. Upon accepting the invitation, the girl is led to a mountain chamber, where she stands in as godparent but is asked to stay for three days. Yet is it really three days that the girl has stayed with the elves where time passes with happiness and pleasure?

The Ugly Duckling

Hans Christian Andersen

Early that morning, a farmer came by, and when he saw how things were, he went out on the pond, broke away the ice with his wooden shoe, and carried the duckling home to his wife. There, the duckling revived, but when the children wished to play with him, <u>he</u> thought they meant to hurt <u>him</u>. Terrified, he fluttered into the milk pail, splashing the whole room with milk. The woman shrieked and threw up her hands as he flew into the butter tub and then in and out of the meal barrel. Imagine what he looked like now! The woman screamed and lashed out at him with the fire tongs. The children tumbled over one another as they tried to catch him, and they laughed, and they shouted. Luckily, the door was open, and the duckling escaped through it into the bushes, where he lay down in the newly fallen snow as if in a daze.

But it would be too sad to tell of all the hardships and wretchedness he had to endure during this cruel winter. When the warm sun shone once more, the duckling was still alive among the reeds of the marsh. The larks began to sing again. It was beautiful springtime.

Then, quite suddenly, he lifted his wings. <u>They</u> swept through the air much more strongly than before, and their powerful strokes carried him far. Before he quite knew what was happening, he found himself in a great garden where apple trees bloomed. The lilacs filled the air with sweet scent and hung in clusters from long, green branches that bent over a winding stream. Oh, but it was lovely here in the freshness of spring!

From the thicket before him came three lovely white swans. They ruffled their feathers and swam lightly in the stream. The duckling recognised these noble creatures, and a strange feeling of sadness came upon him.

"I shall fly neat these royal birds, and they will peck me to bits because I, who am so very ugly, dare to go near them. But I don't care. Better be killed by them than to be nipped by the ducks, pecked by the hens, kicked about by the hen-yard girl, or suffer such misery in winter."

Answer the following questions.

1. The farmer broke away the ice with _____ _____ _____.

2. Who is "he" (in the third line) and "him" (in the fourth line) of the first paragraph referring to?

3. What did the duckling do to make the wife of the farmer really mad?

4. How did the duckling escape?

5. Which phrase (three words in the first paragraph) tells us that the duckling didn't really know what was happening?

6. What suggests that springtime had arrived?

7. What is "they" in the first line of the third paragraph referring to?

8. Where did the duckling land?

9. Which word in the third paragraph tells us that the stream was not straight?

10. The duckling felt _____ when he recognised the noble creatures.
    a. melancholy
    b. misunderstood
    c. lost

11. If the worst were to happen, the duckling chose to be
    a. killed by the royal birds.
    b. nipped by the ducks.
    c. pecked by the hens.
    d. kicked about by the hen-yard girl.

Read on:

'The Ugly Duckling' is a fairy tale by Hans Christian Andersen, a Danish poet and author. The duckling is so called because he is born looking different from his siblings and, for that reason, he is ridiculed and bullied mercilessly. The Ugly Duckling wishes he were beautiful like the swans he sees flying gracefully and majestically in the sky. He indeed turns into one when he grows and matures by the end of the story.

Morals of the story: accept others for their qualities and their unique values and not to judge others by their looks.

Snow White and the Seven Dwarfs

The Brothers Grimm

"I would like very much to buy your apple," said Snow White. "But I have no money."

"That fine comb in your hair will make a good trade," said the old woman.

"Well, all right then!" said Snow White. She took the comb out of her hair and gave it to the old woman, who then gave her the apple. Snow White took a big bite. Alas, the fruit was poisoned! At once, Snow White fell to the ground in a deep sleep.

"YES!" shouted the Queen, <u>pumping the air with her fists</u>.

Just then, the door flew open. In marched the Seven Dwarfs, home from the day's work. Shocked indeed they were to find Snow White lying on the floor and what had to be her stepmother beside her, laughing!

They chased that evil Queen out the door and into the storm. Up to the very top of a mountain, they chased her. All of a sudden, lightning hit the mountain! The Queen fell, and she was never seen again.

But there was nothing to help poor Snow Shite. She stayed absolutely still in her deep sleep. The Seven Dwarfs gently lifted her into a glass coffin. Day and night, they kept watch over her.

One day the Prince happened to pass through. Ever since he had learned that Snow White was missing at the castle, he was searching for her, far and wide. Now he had finally found her but in such a state! The Prince pulled open the glass coffin. Her face seemed so fresh, even in that deep sleep.

He gently took one of Snow White's hands in his own and kissed <u>it</u>. At once, Snow White's eyes opened! With love's first kiss, the evil Queen's spell was forever gone. Now nothing stood in the way for Snow White and the Prince to be together forever. They returned to the kingdom and lived happily ever after.

Answer the following questions.

1. Snow White could not buy the apple because she had _____ _____.

2. Underline the phrase (four words within the first three paragraphs) which means "make a good bargain".

3. Write two sentences with the word "bite" as a noun and as a verb.
   1. Noun: _____
   2. Verb: _____

4. What happened to Snow White when she took a bite of the apple?

5. The expression "pumping the air with her fists" means the queen was
   a. very unsatisfied
   b. very energetic
   c. very happy

6. What did the Seven Dwarfs see when they returned home from work?

7. Number the following sentences in the right sequence:
   _____ The Seven Dwarfs chased the Queen up to the mountain.
   _____ The Queen fell to her death.
   _____ The Seven Dwarfs chased the evil Queen out the door.
   _____ The Seven Dwarfs chased the evil Queen into the storm.

8. Where would the body of the Queen be found?

9. The Seven Dwarfs placed Snow White in a _____ _____.

10. Underline the phrase (three words in the second last paragraph) that means "everywhere".

11. The pronoun "it" in the second line of the last paragraph is referring to

   _____.

12. Was it a good or sad ending to the story? Why do you say that?

Read on:

First published in 1812 in the edition of Grimm's Fairy Tales, the story tells of Snow White's jealous stepmother, the queen, who plots to remain proclaimed the fairest one of all. When Snow White flees into the forest to be away from her stepmother, she encounters the Seven Dwarfs whom she befriends. The princess is then tricked by the Evil Queen-turned-vendor with a poisoned apple, the magic of which only a true lover's kiss can break.

'Snow White and the Seven Dwarfs' remains one of the most widely known 19th century German fairy tales across the Western world.

Hansel and Gretel

The Brothers Grimm

"Fool," said the woman. "That is not your little pigeon, that is the morning sun that is shining on the chimney."

Hansel, however, little by little, threw all the crumbs on the path. The woman led the children still deeper into the forest, where they had never in their lives been before.

Then a great fire was again made, and the mother said, "Just sit there, you children, and when you are tired, you may sleep a little. We are going into the forest to cut wood, and in the evening, when we are done, we will come and fetch you away."

When it was noon, Gretel shared her piece of bread with Hansel, who had scattered his by the way. Then they fell asleep, and evening passed, but no one came to the poor children.

They did not awake until it was dark night, and Hansel comforted his little sister and said, "Just wait, Gretel, until the moon rises, and then we shall see the crumbs of bread which I have strewn about. They will show us our way home again."

When the moon came, they set out, but they found no crumbs, for the many thousands of birds, which fly about in the woods and fields, had picked them all up. Hansel said to Gretel, "We shall soon find the way."

But they did not find it. They walked the whole night and all the next day too, from morning 'til evening, but they did not get out of the forest and were very hungry, for they had nothing to eat but two or three berries, which grew on the ground. And as they were so weary that their legs would carry them no longer, they lay down beneath a tree and fell asleep.

It was now three mornings since they had left their father's house. They began to walk again, but they always came deeper into the forest, and if help did not come soon, they must die of hunger and weariness. When it was midday, they saw a beautiful snow-white bird sitting on a bough, which sang so delightfully that they stood still and listened to it. And when its song was over, it spread its wings and flew away before them, and they followed it until they reached a little house, on the roof of which it alighted. And when they approached the little house, they saw that it was built of bread and covered with cakes, but that the windows were of clear sugar.

Answer the following questions.

1. True or False:
   Hansel threw all the crumbs on the path all at once. _____
   Which three words support your answer?

2. Were the children familiar with where they were in the forest? How do you know?

3. What did the mother say they were going to do?
   She said that _____.

4. Why did Gretel share her bread with Hansel?

5. Underline the correct word:
   Every day we pass/past by the bakery.
   Every day we walk pass/past the bakery.

6. When and how would the two children make their way home?

7. The children couldn't find crumbs along the way they came because
   a. the crumbs had been picked by ants.
   b. the crumbs had been picked up by birds.
   c. there was no moon that night.

8. Was Hansel confident that they would find their way home? How do you know?

9. Hansel and Gretel had nothing to eat but some _____, which grew on the _____.

10. Underline the part of the sentence in the seventh paragraph that tells us that the two children were too tired to walk any farther.

11. If help did not come, the two children might die of _____ and _____.
    a. hopelessness
    b. lack of food
    c. tiredness
    d. fear

12. Describe the house the children finally came upon.

Read on:

After being abandoned by their parents, Hansel and Gretel walk along, not knowing what fortune or fate has in store for them.

At the end of this 200-year-old Grimm fairy tale, the brother and sister escape from the imprisonment of the wicked witch they have come upon and return home happy and rich with the witch's priceless stones.

The Frog Princess

The Brothers Grimm

In days gone by, there was a King who had three sons. When his sons came of age, the King called them to him and said, "My dear lads, I want you to get married so that I may see your little ones, my grandchildren, before I die."

And his sons replied, "Very well, Father, give us your blessing. To whom do you want us to marry?"

"Each of you must take an arrow, go out into the green meadow and shoot it. Where the arrows fall, there shall your destiny be."

So the sons bowed to their father, and each of them took an arrow and went out into the green meadow, where they drew their bows and let fly their arrows.

The arrow of the eldest son fell in the courtyard of a nobleman, and the nobleman's daughter picked it up. The arrow of the middle son fell in the yard of a merchant, and the merchant's daughter picked it up. But the arrow of the youngest son, Prince Ivan, flew up and away he knew not where. He walked on and on in search of it, and at last, he came to a marsh, where what should he see but a frog sitting on a lead with the arrow in its mouth. Prince Ivan said to it, "Frog, Frog, give me back my arrow."

And the frog replied, "Marry me!"

"How can I marry a frog?"

"Marry me, for it is your destiny."

Prince Ivan was sadly disappointed, but what could he do? He picked up the frog and brought it home. The King celebrated three weddings: his eldest son was married to the nobleman's daughter, his middle son to the merchant's daughter, and poor Prince Ivan to the frog.

Answer the following questions.

1. Underline the phrase (three words in the first paragraph) which means "became old enough."

2. Why did the King want his three sons to get married?

3. Where did the boys have to go to shoot their arrows?

4. Which of the following answers is wrong? The three boys bowed to their father before they left
   a. to show respect.
   b. to say sorry.
   c. to get his blessing.

5. What did the boys have to do before they could shoot their arrows?

6. Underline the phrase (four words in the fifth paragraph) which means "looking for it."

7. Where did the youngest prince finally find the arrow?

8. The word "destiny" means
   a. fortune
   b. luck
   c. fate
   d. idea

9. Why was Prince Ivan sadly disappointed?

10. This kind of story is called
    a. a diary
    b. a fairy tale
    c. a memoir

Read on:

'The Frog Princess' is a fairy tale that has various versions with Russian, Norwegian, and other origins.

The story begins with the king wanting his three sons to get married. He tells each prince to shoot an arrow in a different direction and where the arrow lands is where the prince will find his bride. Believe it or not, the youngest prince's arrow is picked up by a frog put under a magical spell.

Perseus the Hero

Nadia Higgins

A feast and sports were going on when they got there, and beside the king of the land sat Acrisius, an aged man, yet a kingly one indeed.

And Perseus thought, *If I, a stranger, take part in the sports and carry away prizes from the men of Larissa, surely the heart of Acrisius must soften towards me.*

Thus did he take off his helmet and cuirass and stood unclothed beside the youths of Larissa, and so godlike was he that they all said, amazed, "Surely this stranger comes from Olympus and is one of the Immortals."

In his hand, he took a discus, and full five fathoms beyond those of the others he cast it, and a great shout arose from those who watched, and Acrisius cried out as loudly as all the rest.

"Further still!" they cried. "Further still canst thou hurl! thou art a hero indeed!"

And Perseus, putting forth all his strength, hurled once again, and the discus flew from his hand like a bolt from the hand of Zeus. The watchers held their breath and made ready for a shout of delight as they saw it speed on, further than mortal man had ever hurled before. But joy died in their hearts when a gust of wind caught the discus as it sped and hurled it against Acrisius, the king. And with a sigh like the sigh that passes through the leaves of a tree as the woodman fells it and it crashed to the earth, so did Acrisius fall and lie prone. To his side rushed Perseus and lifted him tenderly in his arms. But the spirit of Acrisius had fled. And with a great cry of sorrow, Perseus called to the people, "Behold me! I am Perseus, grandson of the man I have slain! Who can avoid the decree of the gods?"

For many a year thereafter, Perseus reigned as a king, and to him and to his fair wife were born four sons and three daughters. Wisely and well he reigned, and when, at a good old age, Death took him and the wife of his heart.

Answer the following questions.

1. The king and Acrisius were enjoying _____ _____ and _____ on this special day.

2. Was Acrisius a young man? How do you know?

3. What did Perseus want to achieve by taking part in the sports?

4. Which word in the third paragraph tells us that Perseus looks like one of the Immortals?

5. How far did Perseus cast the discus?

6. How do we know Acrisius was very impressed by the performance of Perseus?

7. Give three examples of words that are of old English.

8. The discus that flew in the air was compared to _____ _____. This literary device is called
   a. simile
   b. metaphor
   c. repetition

9. Underline the part of the sentence in the sixth paragraph that means "the spectators were in a state of suspense and anticipation."

10. True or False:
    a. Acrisius was killed by the sighing of the wind. _____
    b. Acrisius was killed by the discus. _____
    c. Acrisius was killed by a falling tree. _____

11. The sentence "To his side rushed Perseus" is an example of a literary device called alliteration/inversion. The sentence would be better understood if it were written "Perseus _____ _____ _____ _____."

12. The sentence "But the spirit of Acrisius had fled." means Acrisius _____ _____.

Read on:

The son of Zeus and Danae, Perseus, is the Greek hero best known for his heroic feats petrifying Medusa and rescuing Andromeda from a sea monster.

In this part of the story, Perseus is invited to participate in funeral games in honor of the king, his grandfather, Acrisius. Perseus, with his discus, accidentally hits his grandfather who is watching the games. With the death of Acrisius, the prophesy that his death will be caused by his grandson is fulfilled. The story ends with Perseus inheriting the throne of Argo.

The Life and Adventures of Santa Claus

L. Frank Baum

Those were happy days for Claus when he carried his accumulation of toys to the children who had awaited them so long. During his imprisonment in the Valley, he had been so industrious that all his shelves were filled with playthings, and after quickly supplying the little ones living nearby, he saw he must now extend his travels to wider fields.

Remembering the time when he had journeyed with Ak through all the world, he knew children were everywhere, and he longed to make as many as possible happy with gifts.

So he loaded a great sack with all kinds of toys, slung it upon his back that he might carry it more easily, and started off on a longer trip than he had yet undertaken.

Wherever he showed his merry face, in hamlet or in farmhouse, he received a cordial welcome, for his fame had spread into far lands. At each village, the children swarmed about him, following his footsteps wherever he went; and the women thanked him gratefully for the joy he brough their little ones; and the men looked upon him curiously that he should devote his time to such a queer occupation as toy-making. But every one smiled on him and gave him kindly words, and Claus felt amply repaid for his long journey.

When the sack was empty, he went back again to the Laughing Valley and once more filled it to the brim. This time he followed another road, into a different part of the country, and carried happiness to many children who never before had owned a toy or guessed that such a delightful plaything existed.

After a third journey, so far away that Claus was many days walking the distance, the store of toys became exhausted, and without delay, he set about making a fresh supply.

Answer the following questions.

1. Which word in the first line of this story tells us that Santa Claus had been collecting toys for a while?

2. During his time in the Valley, Claus had been
   a. enjoying life
   b. working hard
   c. doing housework

3. To whom did Claus give his toys first?

4. True or False:
   a. Claus always travelled alone around the world. _____
   b. Claus knew his toys would make children happy. _____

5. Give two reasons why Claus had to carry the great sack of toys upon his back?

6. The word _____ found in the fourth paragraph tells us that many, many children surrounded Claus where he appeared.

7. Match the following sentences to make them correct:
   a. The children   wondered why Claus made toys for an occupation.
   b. The women   followed Claus wherever he went.
   c. The men   welcomed Claus politely.
   d. Everyone   thanked Claus with gratitude.

8. Underline the two words in the fourth paragraph that show Claus felt rewarded significantly.

9. How do we know the Valley might actually be a happy and fun place?

10. Did Claus always follow the same road to where he wanted to go? Find evidence in the passage to support your answer.

11. Who were the children that appreciated the toys the most?

12. We know Claus travelled on foot/on horseback/by boat because according to the passage, he _____ _____ _____.

Read on:

In the Laughing Valley, Santa Claus has become known for his benevolence towards children. Yet with the children's toys which can keep them from misbehaving being stolen by some invisible evil beings, Santa Claus decides to make journeys by night and enters houses with locked doors through chimneys. As Claus's journeys continue, he is aided by two deer named Glossie and Flossie, who pull his sleigh full of toys to different homes in different lands.

The Terrible Olli

A Fairy Tale from Finland

There was once a wicked rich old Troll who lived on a Mountain that sloped down to a Bay. A decent Finn, a farmer, lived on the opposite side of the Bay. The farmer had three sons. When the boys had reached manhood, he said to them one day, "I should think it would shame you three strong youths that that wicked old Troll over there should live on year after year and no one trouble him. We work hard like honest Finns and are as poor at the end of the year as at the beginning. That old Troll, with all his wickedness, grows richer and richer. I tell you, if you boys had any real spirit, you'd take his riches from him and drive him away!"

His youngest son, whose name was Olli, at once cried out, "Very well, Father, I will!"

But the two older sons, offended at Olli's promptness, declared, "You'll do no such thing! Don't forget your place in the family! You're the youngest, and we're not going to let you push us aside. Now, Father, we two will go across the Bay and rout out that old Troll. Olli may come with us, if he likes, and watch us while we do it."

Olli laughed and said, "All right!" for he was used to his brothers treating him like a baby.

So in a few days, the three brothers walked around the Bay and up the Mountain and presented themselves at the Troll's house. The Troll and his old wife were at home. They received the brothers with great civility.

"You're the sons of the Finn who lives across the Bay, aren't you?" the Troll said. "I've watched you boys grow up. I am certainly glad to see you, for I have three daughters who need husbands. Marry my daughters, and you'll inherit my riches."

The old Troll made this offer to get the young men into his power.

"Be careful!" Olli whispered.

But the brothers were too delighted at the prospect of inheriting the Troll's riches so easily to pay any heed to Olli's warning. Instead, they accepted the Troll's offer at once.

Answer the following questions.

1. Two adjectives to describe old Troll are _____ and _____.

2. A synonym for the word "decent" is
    a. proper
    b. dishonest
    c. immoral

3. Underline the three words in the first paragraph that suggest that the three sons of Finn were old enough to get married.

4. What were two complaints Finn was making against the old Troll?

5. The youngest son, Olli, said, "Very well, Father, I will!" What would he do?

6. Underline the sentence (seven words) that implies the two elder brothers were offended by Olli's disrespect for them.

7. True or False:
    a. The two elder sons appeared to be on the same side. _____
    b. The two elder sons felt that they were being pushed around by their little brother. _____

8. Underline the phrase (three words in the fifth paragraph) that means much courtesy and fine manners.

9. What was Troll's real intention offering his daughters to the three boys?

10. Why were the two elder brothers so eager to accept Troll's proposal?

11. Put the following descriptions in the correct sequence:
    _____ The three brothers listened to their father's ranting.
    _____ The three brothers arrived at Troll's house.
    _____ The two brothers agreed to marry Troll's daughters.
    _____ The two brothers asked Olli to learn from them.

12. This story is an example of a
    a. fantasy
    b. horror story
    c. folklore

Read on:

'The Terrible Olli', a Finnish fairy tale by Parker Fillmore, depicts the rivalry between the honest Finn and a wicked Troll. When the three sons of the decent farmer have grown old enough, they are sent by their righteous father to drive away the wicked old Troll who lives in the mountain on the other side of the bay.

Not having a fear in the world, the youngest boy, Olli, tricks the Troll and his wife time and again and eventually proves himself to be the terrible Olli that no Trolls ever dare to settle nearby again.

My Father's Dragon

My Father Finds the Island
Ruth Stiles Gannett

My father hid in the hold for six days and nights. Twice, he was nearly caught when the ship stopped to take on more cargo. But at least he heard a sailor say that the next port would be Cranberry and that they'd be unloading the wheat there. My father knew the sailors would send him home if they caught him, so he looked in his knapsack and took out a rubber band and the empty grain bag with the label saying "Cranberry." At the last moment, my father got inside the bag, knapsack and all, folded the top of the bag inside, and put the rubber band around the top. He didn't look just exactly like the other bags, but it was the best he could do.

Soon the sailors came to unload. They lowered a big net into the hold and began moving the bags of wheat. Suddenly, one sailor yelled, "Great Scott! This is the queerest bag of wheat I've ever seen! It's all lumpy-like, but the label says it's to go to Cranberry."

The other sailors looked at the bag too, and my father, who was in the bag, of course, tried even harder to look like a bag of wheat. Then another sailor felt the bag, and he just happened to get hold of my father's elbow. "I know what this is," he said. "This is a bag of dried corn on the cob," and he dumped my father into the big net along with the bags of wheat.

This all happened in the late afternoon, so late that the merchant in Cranberry who had ordered the wheat didn't count his bags until the next morning. He was a very punctual man and never late for dinner. The sailors told the captain, and the captain wrote down on a piece of paper that they had delivered one hundred and sixty bags of wheat and one bag of dried corn on the cob. They left the piece of paper for the merchant and sailed away that evening.

Answer the following questions.

1. How many times was the writer's father almost caught when he was on the ship?

2. Underline the correct answers:
   Cranberry could be a mountain/port or a fruit/vegetable.

3. Why was the writer's father worried that he would be found by the sailors?

4. What would the bag of the writer's father have looked like it was holding if he had done a great job?

5. "Great Scott!" is an example of
   a. adjective
   b. adverb
   c. conjunction
   d. interjection

6. Underline the sentence that implies that the sailor was suspicious of what was in the bag.

7. What did the writer's father do in the bag to reduce the suspicion of the sailor?

8. What did one of the sailors decide the bag was holding?

9. Because the merchant was never late for dinner, he could be described as a _____ man.

10. Do you think the merchant could ever find the bag of dried corn on the cob? Why or why not?

11. Arrange the following sentences in the correct sequence:

    _____ The sailors moved the bags of wheat with a big net.
    _____ The captain wrote down the number of bags of produce.
    _____ The writer's father hid inside an empty bag he took out from his knapsack.
    _____ One sailor announced that one of the bags was dried corn on the cob.

Read on:

In this part of the story, Elmer is determined to save the baby dragon enslaved by the local merchants. He sneaks aboard a ship and sets out to sea. Hiding in a sack and pretending to be a bag of wheat, Elmer arouses the suspicion of a few sailors, but Elmer manages to escape once the ship docks.

Firmly set to complete his special mission, Elmer ventures through the forest, where he succeeds in tricking some hostile and moody beasts, rescues the dragon from a fantasy island and makes a new but lasting friendship.

Some prominent themes of this story are determination, bravery and resourcefulness.

Theme in Yellow

Carl Sandberg

I spot the hills

With yellow balls in autumn.

I light the prairie cornfields

Orange and tawny gold clusters

And I am called pumpkins.

On the last of October

When dusk is fallen

Children join hands

And circle round me

Singing ghost songs

And love to the harvest moon;

I am a jack-o'-lantern

With terrible teeth

And the children know

I am fooling.

Answer the following questions.

1. How many stanzas are there in this poem?

2. "I spot the hills . . ." What is "I" in this poem referring to?

3. This poem is written from the point of view of
    a. the first person
    b. the second person
    c. the third person

4. What are the three colours mentioned in this poem?

5. Colours appeal to our sense of
    a. seeing
    b. hearing
    c. touching

6. When do the children gather around the jack-o'-lantern?

7. What songs do they sing?

8. What season of the year is this poem set? Give evidence.

9. Which line tells us that the children are not afraid of the jack-o'-lantern with terrible teeth?

10. Which is <u>not</u> the meaning of "I am fooling" in the last line?
    a. I am not serious
    b. I am not harmful
    c. I am a fool
    d. I am fun-loving

Read on:

Written in "common folk language" by Carl Sandberg and published in 1916, the poem 'Theme in Yellow' offers a first-person perspective of the pumpkin-speaker who conveys messages related to the beauty of the natural world of autumn and the games children play in celebration of Halloween.

On Halloween night, young folks come together, join hands, and sing ghost songs around the pumpkin, which is a jack-o'-lantern with terrible teeth and which the children are not afraid of. 'Theme in Yellow,' light-hearted and fun in mood, is written in free verse with no rhyme scheme. The title of the poem itself is a symbolic representation of the season in which the shades of yellow dominate.

Prince Hyacinth and the Dear Little Princess

(The Blue Fairy Book)
Andrew Lang

Once upon a time, there lived a king who was deeply in love with a princess, but she could not marry anyone because she was under an enchantment. So the king set out to seek a fairy and asked what he could do to win the princess's love.

The fairy said to him, "You know that the princess has a great cat which she is very fond of. Whoever is clever enough to tread on that cat's tail is the man she is destined to marry."

The king said to himself that this would not be very difficult, and he left the fairy, <u>determined</u> to grind the cat's tail to powder rather than not tread on it at all.

You may imagine that it was not long before he went to see the princess, and puss, as usual, marched in before him, arching his back. The king took a long step and quite thought he had the tail under his foot, but the cat turned round so sharply that he only trod on air. And so it went on for eight days 'til the king began to think that this fatal tail must be full of quicksilver—it was never still for a moment.

At last, however, he was lucky enough to come upon puss fast asleep and with his tail conveniently spread out. So the king, without losing a moment, set his foot upon it heavily.

With one terrific yell, the cat sprang up and instantly changed into a tall man, who, fixing his angry eyes upon the king, said, "You shall marry the princess because you have been able to break the enchantment, but I will have my revenge. You shall have a son, who will never be happy until he finds out that his nose is too long, and if you ever tell anyone what I have just said to you, you shall vanish away instantly, and no one shall ever see you or hear of you again."

Though the king was horribly afraid of the enchanter, he <u>could not help</u> laughing at this threat.

"If my son has such a long nose as that," he said to himself, "he must always see it or feel it, at least, if he is not blind or without hands."

27

Answer the following questions.

1. Why couldn't the princess marry anyone?

2. Find the word that means "step" in the first two paragraphs.

3. To marry the princess, one has to walk on the cat's
   a. hand
   b. paws
   c. tail

4. The word "determined" in the third paragraph means
   a. decided doubtfully
   b. decided firmly
   c. decided quickly

5. What happened when the king tried to step on the cat's tail?

6. Quicksilver is another term for gold/silver/bronze/mercury.

7. Why was the tail of the cat described to be full of quicksilver?

8. Did the king move fast enough to step on the cat's tail when it was sleeping? Which four words support your answer?

9. Was the tall man the cat turned into happy that the spell was undone? Give two pieces of evidence to support your answer.

10. The tall young man was probably
    a. a witch
    b. a wizard

11. Make a sentence with the word "help" as used in the second last paragraph.
    I could not help _____ when _____.

12. The king was not worried about the curse cast on his son because his son would be able to tell he had a long nose unless he was _____ and had no _____.

Read on:

'Prince Hyacinth and the Dear Little Princess' is a French fairy tale, one of the stories in Andrew Lang's *The Blue Fairy Book*. The story tells of a king who is deeply in love with a princess. Yet because of an ogre's spell, the princess cannot marry anyone. Later in the story, the king happens to offend the ogre, and the princess he eventually marries gives birth to a son with a nose as big as a melon. The queen mother subsequently orders that all members of the royal court must wear fake noses matching her son's.

Building of the Wall

A Norse Legend

Always there had been war between the Giants and the Gods—between the Giants who would have destroyed the world and the race of men and the Gods who would have protected the race of men and would have made the world more beautiful.

There are many stories to be told about the Gods, but the first one that should be told to you is the one about the building of their City.

The Gods had made their way up to the top of a high mountain, and there, they decided to build a great City for themselves that the Giants could never overthrow. The City they would call Asgard, which means the Place of the Gods. They would built it on a beautiful plain on the top of that high mountain. And they wanted to raise round their City the highest and strongest wall that had ever been built.

Now one day, when they were beginning to build their halls and their palaces, a strange being came to them. Odin, the Father of the Gods, went and spoke to <u>him</u>. "What dost thou want on the Mountain of the Gods?" he asked the Stranger.

"I know what is in the mind of the Gods," the Stranger said. "They would build a City here. I cannot build palaces, but I can build great walls that can never be overthrown. Let me build the wall round your City."

"How long will it take to build a wall that will go round our City?" said the Father of the Gods.

"A year, O Odin," said the Stranger.

Now Odin knew, if a great wall could be built around it, the Gods would not have to spend all their time defending their City, Asgard, from the Giants, and he knew, if Asgard were protected, he himself could go amongst men and teach them and help them. He thought no payment the Stranger could ask would be too much for the building of that wall.

Answer the following questions.

1. True or False:
   a. There had always been peace between the Giants and the Gods. _____
   b. The Giants and the Gods wanted to do good to the world. _____

2. What had the Gods always wanted to do for the world?

3. The word _____ is a synonym for "conquer" found in the third paragraph of the story.

4. The great city on the top of the mountain
   a. is called Asgard.
   b. means the Place of the Goddesses.
   c. is built on a beautiful plain.

5. Why would the Gods want to raise round the city the highest and strongest walls?

6. The pronoun "him" in the fourth paragraph is referring to the _____.

7. Suggest two words in the fourth paragraph that are old English words.

8. The phrase "in the minds of the Gods" means I know what the Gods
   _____ _____.

9. Arrange the following sentences in the correct sequence:
   _____ Odin considered the Stranger's promise seriously.
   _____ A stranger offered to build the wall round the city.
   _____ The God began with building the walls and palaces.
   _____ The God made their way to the top of a high mountain to build a great city for themselves.

10. What would Odin want to do if Asgard were protected?

11. Which line in the last paragraph suggests that Odin was ready to pay however much Asgard asked of him?

12. Is this story fiction or nonfiction? Explain.

Read on:

'Building of the Wall' is an illustrated story of Nordic origin for children. In the story, Odin, the Father of the Woods, wants a high, protective wall to be built around the city, Asgard, which is the celestial stronghold of the Aesir tribe of gods and goddesses. It is meant to protect the inhabitants of the city against the invasion by the giants and other beings that are the gods' enemies. A smith, a master builder, who comes from the lands of giants, arrives one day and promises to finish building the wall in one year. In return, he wants the sun, the moon, and the Goddess Freya as his wife for payment.

Rumpelstiltskin

The Brothers Grimm

And when the king came in the morning and found all as he had wished, he took her in marriage, and the pretty miller's daughter became a queen.

A year after, she brought a beautiful child into the world, and she never gave a thought to the manikin. But suddenly, he came into her room and said, "Now give me what you promised."

The queen was horror-struck and offered the manikin all the riches of the kingdom if he would leave her the child. But the manikin said, "No, something alive is dearer to me than all the treasures in the world."

Then the queen began to lament and cry so that the manikin pitied her.

"I will give you three days' time," said he, "and if by that time you find out my name, then shall you keep your child."

So the queen thought the whole night of all the names she had ever heard, and she sent a messenger over the country, far and wide, to enquire for any other names there might be. When the manikin came the next day, she began with Caspar, Melchior, Balthazar, and said all the names she knew, one after another, but to everyone, the little man said, "That is not my name."

On the second day, she had enquiries made in the neighbourhood as to the names of the people there, and she repeated to the manikin the most uncommon and curious. Perhaps your name is Shortribs or Sheepshanks or Laceleg, but he always answered, "That is not my name."

On the third day, the messenger came back again and said, "I have not been able to find a single new name, but as I came to a high mountain at the end of the forest, where the fox and the hare bid each other good night, there I saw a little house, and before the house, a fire was burning, and round about the fire, quite a ridiculous little man was jumping. He hopped upon one leg and shouted,

"To-day I bake, to-morrow brew,
the next I'll have the young queen's child.
Ha, glad am I that no one knew
that Rumpelstiltskin I am styled."

Answer the following questions.

1. When the king married the pretty miller's daughter, the latter became _____ _____.

2. What added to the joy of the king and queen a year later?

3. The phrase "never gave a thought to" means the queen had
   a. never dreamed of
   b. never gave anything to
   c. completely forgotten about

4. A word in the third passage that means "overwhelmed by terror" is _____.

5. What did the queen offer to the manikin for her child? Was she successful?

6. If the answer were "no" to question 5, why didn't the manikin take the offer?

7. Underline the phrase (three words between paragraphs 2 and 4) that suggests the queen was very sad.

8. What did the queen have to do to keep the child?

9. Shortribs and sheepshanks are examples of names that are
   a. most common in modern times
   b. most uncommon and curious
   c. most predictable and popular

10. What did the messenger see at the end of the forest?

11. The repetition of the letter "b" in the sentence, "To-day I <u>b</u>ake, to-morrow <u>b</u>rew" is an example of
    a. rhyme
    b. simile
    c. alliteration

12. Can you tell the name of the manikin? If so, what is it?

Read on:

'Rumplestiltskin' is a German fairy tale collected by the Brothers Grimm in their collection of fairy tales. The name Rumplestiltskin in German literally means "little rattle stilt." In the story, when Rumplestiltskin comes for the queen's baby, he allows the devastated mother three days to figure out his name to be able to keep her child. On the third day, a song that Rumplestiltskin sings and reveals his name is heard by a queen's messenger.

The Story of the Merchant and the Genius

From One Thousand and One Nights

"Sire, there was once upon a time a merchant who possessed great wealth, in land and merchandise, as well as in ready money. He was obliged from time to time to take journeys to arrange his affairs. One day, having to go a long way from home, he mounted his horse, taking with him a small wallet in which he had put a few biscuits and dates because he had to pass through the desert where no food was to be got. He arrived without any mishap and, having finished his business, set out on his return. On the fourth day of his journey, the heat of the sun being very great, he turned out of his road to rest under some trees. He found at the foot of a large walnut tree a fountain of clear and running water. He <u>dismounted</u>, fastened his horse to a branch of the tree, and sat by the fountain, after having taken from his wallet of his dates and biscuits. When he had finished this <u>frugal meal,</u> he washed his face and hands in the fountain.

When he was thus employed, he saw an enormous genius, white with rage, coming towards him with a scimitar in his hand.

'Arise,' he cried in a terrible voice, 'and let me kill you as you have killed my son!'

As he uttered these words, he gave a frightful yell. The merchant, quite as much terrified at the hideous face of the monster at his words, answered him tremblingly, 'Alas, good sire, what can I have done to you to deserve death?'

'I shall kill you,' repeated the genius, 'as you have killed my son.'

'But,' said the merchant, 'how can I have killed your son? I do not know him, and I have never even seen him.'

'When you arrived here, did you not sit down on the ground?' asked the genius. 'And did you not take some dates from your wallet, and whilst cutting them, did not you throw the stones about?'

'Yes,' said the merchant, 'I certainly did so.'

'Then,' said the genius, 'I tell you, you have killed my son, for whilst you were throwing about the stones, my son passed by, and one of them struck him in the eye and killed him. So I shall kill you.'

'Ah, sir, forgive me!' cried the merchant.

'I will have no mercy on you,' answered the genius.

'But I killed your son quite unintentionally, so I implore you to spare my life.'

'No,' said the genius, 'I shall kill you as you killed my son,' and so saying, he seized the merchant by the arm, threw him on the ground and lifted his sabre to cut off his head.

The merchant, protesting his innocence, bewailed his wife and children, and tried pitifully to avert <u>his fate</u>. The genius, with his raised scimitar, waited 'til he had finished, but was not in the least touched."

Answer the following questions.

1. The wealthy merchant possessed _____, _____ and _____ _____.

2. Why did the merchant have to take a bit of food with him before making his trip?

3. Underline the phrase (three words in the first paragraph) that means "with no unlucky accidents."

4. The merchant located some trees to rest under because
   a. he was too tired
   b. he was too hungry
   c. it was too hot

5. An antonym for the word "dismounted" in the first paragraph will be
   a. ascended
   b. descended
   c. disembarked

6. What did the "frugal meal" of the merchant contain?

7. Match the genius with the correct descriptions:

   The genius was
       a. very angry
       b. had no weapons in his hands
       c. speaking with a terrible voice
       d. huge in size
       e. threatening to turn the merchant into a monster

8. What did the genius say that frightened the merchant badly?

9. The genius was so angry and upset with the merchant because the latter was believed to have _____ _____ _____.

10. How did the accident regarding the death of the genius' son come about?

11. Which word suggests that the merchant did not kill the son of the genius on purpose?

12. The merchant tried to avert "his fate" at the end of the story. What was his fate at that moment?

Read on:

Translated by Andrew Long and found in *One Thousand and One Nights*, 'The Story of the Merchant and the Genius' reveals how the son of a genie is accidentally killed by a merchant. The genie gives the merchant a year's time to say his goodbyes to those he knows. Nevertheless, three old men come to help by devising a plan to avert the merchant's death.

The Forest of Lilacs

The Countess of Segur

When Blondine entered the forest, she commenced gathering the beautiful branches of lilacs. She rejoiced in their profusion and delighted in their fragrance.

As she made her selection, it seemed to her that those which were more distant were still more beautiful, so she emptied her apron and her hat, which were full, and filled them again and again.

Blondine had been thus busily occupied for about an hour. She began to suffer from the heat and to feel great fatigue. She found the branches of lilacs heavy to carry and thought it was time to return to the palace. She looked around and saw herself surrounded with lilacs. She called Gourmandinet, but no one replied.

"I have wandered farther than I intended," said Blondine. "I will return at once, though I am very weary. Gourmandinet will hear me and will surely come to meet me."

Blondine walked on rapidly for some time, but she could not find the boundaries of the forest.

Many times she called anxiously upon Gourmandinet, but he did not respond, and at last, she became terribly frightened.

"What will become of me, all alone in this vast forest? What will my poor papa think when I do not return? And Gourmandinet, how will he dare to go back to the palace without me? He will be scolded, perhaps beaten, and all this is my fault because I would leave my carriage to gather lilacs? Unfortunate girl that I am! I shall die of hunger and thirst in this forest if the wolves do not eat me up this night."

Weeping bitterly, Blondine fell on the ground at the foot of a large tree. She wept a long time. At last, her great fatigue mastered her grief. She placed her little head upon her bundle of lilacs and slept peacefully.

Answer the following questions.

1. The first thing Blondine did on entering the forest was _____
   _____.

2. Which word in the first paragraph tells that the lilacs smelled good?

3. What was not a reason for Blondine to return to the palace?
   a. She was busily occupied.
   b. She began to suffer from the heat.
   c. The lilac branches were too heavy to carry.

4. Underline the two sentences in the third paragraph to suggest that Blondine was alone.

5. Which word in the fifth paragraph tells us that Blondine walked very quickly?

6. What was Blondine trying to find as she walked off?

7. When did Blondine start feeling scared?

8. True or False:
   For punishment:
   a. Gourmandinet might be scolded _____
   b. Gourmandinet might be beaten _____
   c. Gourmandinet might be put in jail _____

9. What were three ways Blondine might die of?

10. Arrange the following sentences in the correct sequence:
    _____ Blondine called out for Gourmandinet but nobody answered.
    _____ Blondine felt so tired that she fell asleep.
    _____ Blondine started to worry about her own fate in the forest.
    _____ Blondine got carried away on seeing the beautiful branches of lilacs.

11. What caused Blondine to fall asleep finally?

12. The writer wrote this story to advise/to entertain/to complain.

Read on:

Authored by Comtesse de Segur, the story of 'Forest of Lilacs' is found in the book *Old French Fairy Tales*, which contains five long and intriguing French folktales.

When Blondine enters the forest of lilacs, she starts gathering the fragrant flowers, not knowing the passage of time. Then to her dismay, Blondine realises she is left all alone in the forest. And darkness is falling.

The Tale of Peter Rabbit

Beatrix Potter

Then he tried to find his way straight across the garden, but he became more and more puzzled. Presently, he came to a pond where Mr. McGregor filled his water cans. A white cat was staring at some goldfish; she sat very, very still, but now and then, the tip of her tail twitched as if it were alive. Peter thought it best to go away without speaking to her; he has heard about cats from his cousin, little Benjamin Bunny.

He went back towards the tool shed, but suddenly, quite close to him, he heard the noise of a hoe—*scr-r-ritch, scratch, scratch, scritch.* Peter scuttered underneath the bushes. But presently, as nothing happened, he came out and climbed upon a wheelbarrow and peeped over. The first thing he saw was Mr. McGregor hoeing onions. His back was turned towards Peter, and beyond him was the gate!

Peter got down very quietly off the wheelbarrow and started running as fast as he could go, along a straight walk behind some black currant bushes.

Mr. McGregor caught sight of him at the corner, but Peter did not care. He slipped underneath the gate and was safe at last in the wood outside the garden.

Mr. McGregor hung up the little jacket and the shoes for a scarecrow to frighten the blackbirds.

Peter never stopped running or looked behind him 'til he got home to the big fir tree.

He was so tired that he flopped down upon the nice soft sand on the floor of the rabbit hole and shut his eyes. His mother was busy cooking; she wondered what he had done with his clothes. It was the second little jacket and pair of shoes that Peter had lost in a fortnight!

I am sorry to say that Peter was not very well during the evening.

His mother put him to bed and made some camomile tea, and she gave a dose of it to Peter!

"One tablespoonful to be taken at bedtime."

But Flopsy, Mopsy, and Cottontail had bread and milk and blackberries for supper.

Answer the following questions.

1. Soon Peter Rabbit came to a _____ where Mr. McGregor usually filled his
   _____ _____.

2. Was Peter Rabbit's tail alive? Which two words suggest that?

3. "Scr-r-ritch, scratch, scratch, scritch" were the sounds made by the _____ of Mr.
   McGregor. This literary device is called
   a. rhyme
   b. inversion
   c. onomatopoeia

4. Why couldn't Mr. McGregor see Peter Rabbit climbing upon the wheelbarrow?

5. Why did Peter Rabbit get down very quietly off the wheelbarrow?

6. Underline the phrase that means "saw" (three words in the fourth paragraph).

7. What did Mr. McGregor do with Peter Rabbit's jacket and shoes? Was it a good use of
   the two items? Why?

8. Did Peter Rabbit keep stopping or looking behind him as he ran home? How do you
   know?

9. Which line tells us that Mrs. Rabbit did not know what had happened to Peter Rabbit's
   clothes?

10. True or False:
    a. Peter Rabbit had lost his second jacket and pair of shoes within a month. _____
    b. Peter Rabbit's mother was very, very upset with Peter Rabbit. _____

11. Did Peter Rabbit have a proper dinner that night? What would he have had if he had
    not been naughty?

12. Mrs. Rabbit gave Peter Rabbit camomile tea
    a. to keep him relaxed and sleep better
    b. to treat his cold
    c. to treat his mild skin rash

Read on:

The story of Peter Rabbit, written by English author Beatrix Potter, follows the adventures of
a fearless young rabbit that eventually appears in a total of six books that have sold over 150
million copies.

In this story, Peter Rabbit is seen venturing into the garden of Mr. McGregor again. Being
chased around, the rabbit finally escapes, leaving behind his jacket and shoes which Mr.
McGregor keeps for his scarecrow. Peter returns home, where his mother puts him to bed
instantly with no dinner but just a cupful of camomile tea.

Charlotte's Web

E. B. White

The next day was foggy. Everything on the farm was dripping wet. The grass looked like a magic carpet. The asparagus patch looked like a silver forest.

On foggy mornings, Charlotte's web was truly a thing of beauty. This morning each thin strand was decorated with dozens of tiny beads of water. The web glistened in the light and made a pattern of loveliness and mystery, like a delicate veil. Even Lurvy, who wasn't particularly interested in beauty, noticed the web when he came with the pig's breakfast. He noted how clearly it showed up, and he noted how big and carefully built it was. And then he took another look, and he saw something that made him set his pail down. There, in the centre of the web, neatly woven in block letters, was a message. It said: SOME PIG!

Lurvy felt weak. He brushed his hand across his eyes and stared harder at Charlotte's web. "I'm seeing things," he whispered. He dropped to his knees and uttered a short prayer. Then forgetting all about Wilbur's breakfast, he walked back to the house and called Mr. Zuckerman.

"I think you'd better come down to the pigpen," he said.

"What's the trouble?" asked Mr. Zuckerman. "Anything wrong with the pig?"

"N-not exactly," said Lurvy. "Come and see for yourself."

The two men walked silently down to Wilbur's yard. Lurvy pointed to the spider's web. "Do you see what I see?" he asked.

Zuckerman stared at the writing on the web. Then he murmured the words "Some pig." Then he looked at Lurvy. Then they began to tremble. Charlotte, sleepy after her night's exertions, smiled as she watched. Wilbur came and stood directly under the web.

"Some pig!" muttered Lurvy in a low voice.

"Some pig!" whispered Mr. Zuckerman. They stared and stared for a long time at Wilbur. Then they stared at Charlotte.

"You don't suppose that that spider . . .," began Mr. Zuckerman, but he shook his head and didn't finish the sentence. Instead, he walked solemnly back up to the house and spoke to his wife. "Edith, something has happened," he said in a weak voice. He went into the living room and sat down, and Mrs. Zuckerman followed.

"I've got something to tell you, Edith," he said. "You better sit down." Mrs. Zuckerman sank into a chair. She looked pale and frightened.

Answer the following questions.

1. On the foggy day, the grass looked like a _____ _____ and the asparagus patch looked like a _____ _____.

2. What was the web woven by Charlotte compared to?

3. Underline the sentence in the second paragraph that infers that Lurvy was impressed by Charlotte's web.

4. Match the following descriptions correctly to Lurvy.

    a. felt weak on seeing the web.
    b. stared hard at the web.

    Lurvy   c. knelt and said a prayer.
    d. forgot all about Wilber's breakfast.
    e. walked back to his own shed.

5. Change the following sentence to indirect speech.
    "I think you'd better come down to the pigpen," said Lurvy to Mr. Zuckerman.
    Lurvy told Mr. Zuckerman _____
    _____.

6. Which phrase (five words in the eighth paragraph) suggests Charlotte had worked industriously through the night?

7. Charlotte smiled as Mr. Zuckerman and Lurvy were looking at the web because
    a. she was happy to see them tremble
    b. she was very proud of her masterpiece
    c. she was glad she was able to rest

8. The words "muttered" and "whispered" are better than the word "said" because they reflect how stunned/tired/sleepy the two men were.

9. Mr. Zuckerman said to Lurvy, "You don't suppose that that spider . . ." and didn't finish the sentence. What would he have said if he had finished the sentence?

10. Why did Mr. Zuckerman ask his wife, Edith, to sit down first before he told her what he had seen?

11. Why is "The Miracle" the title of this chapter of Charlotte's Web?

Read on:

Authored by E. B. White, illustrated by Garth Williams, and published in 1952 by Harper and Brothers, *Charlotte's Web* is considered a classic of children's literature, equally enjoyed by adults and children.

Charlotte's Web tells the story of friendship and loyalty between a barn pig, Wilbur, and the spider, Charlotte, who helps her simple-minded but good-natured friend to escape his fate of being slaughtered.

Answers
Note to teachers

1. Some of the questions require students to re-examine the text for answers.
2. Some of the questions require students to think to arrive at an answer.
3. Other questions require common sense and some background knowledge. Answers to these questions are often open-ended (shown as 'multiple answers allowed').

About Angels

1. a. the Bible
2. an angel
3. "I am going to run along the road, miles and miles and miles, until I find an angel."
4. he was wearing trousers/he had trousers (on)/he could wear trousers
5. she had a lame foot
6. 1 2 4 3
7. b. very soon
8. velvet, furs, white plumes, jewels, gold (any three items)
9. stared coldly
10. "Go!" / "Go Now!" / She asked him to go right away.

Buster Bear Has a Fine Time

1. the Great Woods
2. Yes – one edge of the Old Pasture touched one edge of the Green Forest
3. honey
4. Yes – he liked berries of all kinds
5. No – "mumbled"
6. a. happy
7. leaves; green berries; ripe berries
8. "from sheer delight"
9. Mr. Sun had crept out of bed
10. shy; bashful
11. four legs
12. there were berries in the Green Forest and man would like to visit the area to pick them

My Shadow

1. quatrains
2. a. AABB
3. a. first person
4. the shadow
5. Proper children grow slowly but the shadow shoots up and gets little quickly.
6. "make a fool of me"
7. a coward ; it stays so close beside the speaker (like sticking to nursie)

8. c. personification
9. c. I rose and found the shining dew on every buttercup.
10. the sun hasn't come out yet

The Elves and the Servant Girl

1. "industrious"
2. on the great heap in front of the door
3. illiterate
4. They asked the girl to hold a child for them at its christening.
5. Yes – "she consented"
6. a. small, c. elegant, d. beautiful
7. 2 1 4 3
8. d. boredom
9. a. False b. False c. True
10. who she was; what business she had there
11. three days; seven years
12. fantasy

The Ugly Duckling

1. a wooden shoe
2. the duckling
3. He fluttered into the milk pail, splashing the whole room with milk.
4. through the open door
5. "in a daze"
6. The warm sun shone once more./The larks began to sing again.
7. his wings
8. in a great garden where apple trees bloomed
9. "winding"
10. a. melancholy
11. a. killed by the royal birds

Snow White and the Seven Dwarfs

1. no money
2. "make a good trade"
3. a. Take a bite (noun) of this sweet apple.
   b. I bite (verb) my gum a lot when I'm nervous.
   (multiple answers accepted)
4. She fell to the ground in a deep sleep.
5. c. very happy
6. Snow White lying on the ground and what must be her stepmother beside her, laughing
7. 3 4 1 2
8. at the foot of the mountain

9. glass coffin
10. "far and wide"
11. one of Snow White's hands
12. a good ending; Snow White and the Prince returned to the Kingdom and lived happily ever after

Hansel and Gretel

1. False; "little by little"
2. No – it says "where they had never in their lives been before"
3. they were going into the forest to cut wood.
4. Hansel had scattered his by the way
5. pass; past
6. when the moon rose; by seeing/following the crumbs of bread which Hansel had strewn about
7. b. the crumbs had been picked up by birds
8. Yes – Hansel said to Gretel, "We shall soon find the way."
9. berries; ground
10. "they were so weary that their legs would carry them no longer"
11. b. lack of food; c. tiredness
12. little; built of bread; covered with cakes; the windows were of clear sugar

The Frog Princess

1. "came of age"
2. the King wanted to see his little ones, his grandchildren, before he died
3. the green meadow
4. b. to say sorry
5. They had to draw their bows.
6. "in search of it"
7. in the marsh
8. c. fate
9. he had to marry a frog
10. b. a fairy tale

Perseus the Hero

1. a feast; sports
2. No – he's described as "an aged man"
3. to carry away the prizes from the men of Larissa
4. "godlike"
5. full five fathoms beyond those of the others
6. He cried out as loudly as all the rest.
7. canst; thou; art
8. a bolt from the hand of Zeus; a. simile

9. "The watchers held their breath and made ready for a shout of delight"
10. a. False
    b. True
    c. False
11. inversion; rushed to his side
12. had died

The Life and Adventures of Santa Claus

1. "accumulation"
2. b. working hard
3. the little ones living nearby
4. a. False
   b. True
5. so that he might carry it more easily; it would be the longest trip he had ever had
6. swarmed
7. a. The children → followed Claus wherever he went.
   b. The women → thanked Claus with gratitude.
   c. The men → wondered why Claus made toys for an occupation.
   d. Everyone → welcomed Claus politely.
8. "amply repaid"
9. It's called the Laughing Valley after all.
10. No – "He followed another road, into a different part of the country."
11. children who never before had owned a toy or guessed that such a delightful plaything existed
12. on foot; walked the distance

The Terrible Olli

1. wicked; rich
2. a. proper
3. "had reached manhood"
4. year after year, no one troubled him; with all his wickedness, he grew richer and richer
5. take away old Troll's riches from him and drive him away
6. "Don't forget your place in the family."
7. a. True
   b. True
8. "with great civility"
9. to get the young men into his power
10. they were too delighted at the prospect of inheriting Troll's wealth
11. 1 3 4 2
12. c. folklore

My Father's Dragon

1. twice/two times
2. port; fruit
3. he knew the sailors would send him home
4. a bag of wheat
5. d. interjection
6. "This is the queerest bag of wheat I've ever seen!"
7. He tried even harder to look like a bag of wheat.
8. dried corn on the cob
9. punctual
10. No – there wasn't one to begin with
11. 2 4 1 3

Theme in Yellow

1. one
2. a pumpkin/a jack-o'-lantern
3. a. the first person
4. yellow; orange; gold
5. a. seeing
6. on the last of October when dusk is fallen
7. ghost songs
8. autumn; the appearance of the harvest moon
9. "And the children know I am fooling."
10. c. I am a fool

Prince Hyacinth and the Dear Little Princess

1. she was under an enchantment/a spell
2. "tread"
3. c. tail
4. b. decided firmly
5. The cat turned round so sharply that the King trod on air.
6. mercury
7. it moved about so quickly
8. Yes – "without losing a moment"
9. No – he had angry eyes; he intended to take revenge
10. b. a wizard
11. laughing (gerund); I heard his joke last night (multiple answers accepted)
12. blind; hands

Building of the Wall

1. a. False
   b. False
2. to protect the race of men and make the world more beautiful
3. overthrow
4. a. is called Asgard
5. so that men could be kept safe from attack / so that the Gods would not have to spend all their time defending the city
6. stranger / strange being
7. "dost"; "thou"
8. are thinking
9. 4 3 2 1
10. to go amongst men and teach them and help them
11. "He thought that no payment the Stranger could ask would be too much for the building of the wall."
12. fiction – the story is based on imaginary people and events

Rumplestiltskin

1. a/the queen
2. a beautiful child
3. c. completely forgotten about
4. horror-struck
5. all the riches of the kingdom; No
6. he said that something alive was dearer to him than all the treasures in the world
7. "lament and cry"
8. to find out the name of the manikin
9. b. most uncommon and curious
10. a little house ; a fire burning ; a ridiculous little man jumping
11. c. alliteration
12. Yes – "Rumplestiltskin"

The Story of the Merchant and the Genius

1. land; merchandise; ready money
2. he had to pass through the desert where no food was to be got
3. "without any mishap"
4. c. it was too hot
5. a. ascended
6. dates and biscuits
7. a. very angry
   c. speaking with a terrible voice
   d. huge in size

8. He said he was going to kill the merchant.
9. killed his son
10. It happened like this: while the merchant was throwing the stones about, the son of the genius passed by, and one of them struck him in the eye and killed him.
11. "unintentionally"
12. He was to be killed. / He was to die.

Forest of Lilacs

1. to gather/gathering the beautiful branches of lilacs
2. "fragrance"
3. a. She was busily occupied.
4. "She looked around and saw herself surrounded with lilacs. She called Gourmandinet but no one replied."
5. "rapidly"
6. the boundaries of the forest
7. when she called anxiously upon Gourmandinet but he did not respond
8. a. True
   b. True
   c. False
9. hunger ; thirst ; being eaten up by wolves
10. 2 4 3 1
11. her great fatigue / tiredness
12. to entertain

The Tale of Peter Rabbit

1. pond; water-cans
2. No – "as if"
3. hoe; c. onomatopoeia
4. his back was turned towards Peter
5. so as not to alert/alarm Mr. McGregor
6. "caught sight of"
7. He hung up the little jacket and shoes for a scare-crow to frighten the blackbirds.
   Yes – no blackbirds would come
8. No – Peter never stopped running or looked behind him till he got home to the big fir tree
9. "she wondered what he had done with his clothes"
10. a. False
    b. False
11. No – he would have had bread, milk and blackberries
12. a. to keep him relaxed and sleep better

Charlotte's Web

1. magic carpet; silver forest
2. a delicate veil
3. "Even Lurvy, who wasn't particularly interested in beauty, noticed the web when he came with the pig's breakfast."
4. a. felt weak on seeing the web; b. stared hard at the web; c. knelt and said a prayer; d. forgot all about Wilber's breakfast.
5. (that) he thought he'd better go down to the pigpen
6. "sleepy after her night's exertions"
7. b. she was very proud of her masterpiece
8. stunned
9. had spun the words "some pig" on the web
10. he probably worried that his wife, Edith, might feel weak and faint
11. it's a miracle for a spider to spin words on its spider web